"Mark Mattes writes w   with
God often gets reduced t   must
do. God turns all of this on its head. As Luther reminds us God
doesn't want to deal with us in any other way than a promise.
The focus is not on our promises to God (broken as they inevitably are) but on God's sure and certain promise to us, a promise
that God obligates Himself to keep. With scriptural clarity and
pastoral wisdom, Mattes shepherds his readers to look away
from the self to Jesus Christ for He alone is the source and end
of faith. Where our checklists would enslave, He gives rest and
freedom."

**—John T. Pless, Assistant Professor of Pastoral
Ministry and Missions and Director of Field
Education, Concordia Theological Seminary**

"How should Lutherans engage evangelicals? Mark Mattes
has provided us with a helpful guide. There is no checklist of
qualities in our heart that can bring us assurance that we share
in the gift of salvation. If anything, a checklist only reinforces
the incurvation of our heart under the guise of piety. The gift
of Christ in water and the Word does not close the door to
Christian living. It opens it. Conversion is not to be single event,
to which we go back, examining our decision or experience.
Conversion is to be a daily event in which we return to the
Christ given to us in baptism. This is a word that evangelicals
need to hear from Lutherans!"

**—Mark A. Seifrid, Professor of Exegetical
Theology Emeritus, Concordia Seminary**

"The question that hounds many Christians is, 'How do I know
I'm saved?' With masterful brevity as well as clear and creative
writing, Mark Mattes provides the answer. Our assurance is
not our decision or our obedience, but solely and completely
in Christ. His life. His work. His death. His resurrection. For
anyone harassed by doubts of salvation, this book is a Godsend,
a balm to the soul."

—Chad Bird, Scholar in Residence, 1517

"During my time as a campus pastor, I encountered countless students overwhelmed by the relentless checklists imposed on them from all sides - professors, coaches, parents, peers, even their churches. I wish I'd had Mark Mattes' gem of a book back then. *Ditching the Checklist* is accessible, insightful, and genuinely helpful. As a parent with a college-aged child, I've already shared this book with her, hoping it will empower her to navigate her own journey with greater clarity and freedom."

—**Dr. Russell Lackey, Pastor,**
Lutheran Church of the Master

"In this direct and accessible booklet, Mark Mattes goes for the theological jugular. For generations, American Christianity has unwittingly preached a gospel of self—especially the notion of the free will and its supposed power to bring sinners to salvation. Although dressed in religious garb and speaking fondly of Jesus, this 'decision theology' misunderstands faith and its object, Christ, leaving people with nagging doubts. In its place, Mattes offers the gospel truth: sinners have nothing to contribute to salvation, but through Christ, God accomplishes it all, and by the Holy Spirit, God delivers it freely to sinners through sermon and sacrament."

—**The Rev. Christopher Richmann, Ph.D., Pastor,**
St. John Lutheran Church (Coryell City)

DITCHING THE CHECKLIST

Assurance of Salvation
for Evangelicals (& Other Sinners)

—

MARK MATTES

DITCHING THE CHECKLIST

Assurance of Salvation
for Evangelicals (& Other Sinners)

—

MARK MATTES

Published by:
1517 Publishing
PO Box 54032
Irvine, CA 92619-4032

Publisher's Cataloging-In-Publication Data
(Prepared by The Donohue Group, Inc.)

Names: Mattes, Mark C., author.
Title: Ditching the checklist : assurance of salvation for evangelicals (and other sinners) / Mark C. Mattes.
Description: Irvine, CA : 1517 Publishing, [2025] | Includes bibliographical references.
Identifiers: ISBN: 978-1-962654-79-1 (paperback) | 978-1-956658-77-4 (ebook) | 978-1-962654-80-7 (audio)
Subjects: LCSH: Mattes, Mark C.—Religion. | Salvation—Christianity. | Sin—Christianity. | Piety. | God (Christianity)—Love. | BISAC: RELIGION / Christian Theology / Soteriology. | RELIGION / Christian Living / Spiritual Growth. | RELIGION / Christian Theology / General.
Classification: LCC: BT751.3 .M38 2025 | DDC: 234—dc23

Printed in the United States of America.

Cover art by Zachariah James Stuef.

Dedication

This booklet is written to the glory
of God and in memory of the ministries
of Luther Cronrath, Robert Rismiller,
John Beem, and Ron Darge.

Table of Contents

Table of Contents

Prologue

As a teen, I occasionally heard revival preachers who pitched that unless people accepted Jesus as their personal Savior and Lord, they were going to hell. Less often, I heard that if people accepted Jesus as Savior and Lord, they would experience a rewarding, full life in the present. Whether for the fear of hell or the quest for happiness, both approaches motivated me to comply. Unfortunately, my decision for Christ, indeed decisions, for there were more than one, did not yield the desired result. I would feel saved for several hours or days, but inevitably, doubts would set in. Even though I had prayed the "sinner's prayer"[1] with as much sincerity as I could muster, I often felt unsaved. Why didn't my decision for Jesus work? Was there something wrong with me? After all, if I didn't feel saved, surely someone was to blame. It couldn't be Jesus, so it had to be me. I questioned my sincerity, thinking my motives were perhaps not entirely pure. Did I really love Christ, or was I just terrified of hell? Perhaps my decision was not decisive, forceful, or definitive enough. After all, I

---

[1] In a "sinner's prayer," people admit to God that they are sinners, acknowledge that Christ died for them, invite Christ into their hearts, and promise God that they will live a Christian life.

still had sinful thoughts. How could it be possible for me to be reborn and still have wicked thoughts? Was I truly reborn?

If these doubts weren't upsetting enough, my life after accepting Christ wasn't as rosy as some preachers said it should be. I wrestled with all the insecurities with which normal teenagers wrestle.

With Jesus in my life, shouldn't I at least feel more confident? My acne-plagued forehead suggested otherwise. Later in my teenage years, I worried that even if I was momentarily saved, that was no guarantee that I wouldn't sin in the future. Future sins could damn me. Now, that description may come across as over the top: worrying about something that hasn't happened and, in fact, may never happen. But lots of people are worrywarts. I'm one of them. I came close to despairing: was there no way for me to be sure I was saved? It took some study and prayer to see matters in a new light that gave me assurance. This booklet is written to share what I learned in the hope that you, too, can rest secure in God's love.

Our Vulnerabilities

My wrestling over the question of salvation is not atypical for Christians. One Evangelical pastor writes that, due to his anxiety over whether his decision for Jesus took, he asked Jesus into his heart about 5,000 times.[1] He was caught in a trap like mine: are you ever *sorry enough* for your sins? If you aren't, did you truly repent? If you haven't truly repented, then your decision for Christ might be of no avail, and you are lost.

Let's look at this matter with some objectivity. When it comes to any fear, it's the awareness of your vulnerability that gives you something to worry about. We are all mortal. Death could take us at any time. We are sinners and will face God's evaluation (Matt 10:28; Matt 25:46; Rev 21:8). We shouldn't assume with "Mainline Protestants" and "Progressive Evangelicals" that salvation is universal.[2] We know that we must

---

[1] J. D. Greear, *Stop Asking Jesus into Your Heart: How to Know for Sure You Are Saved* (Nashville, TN: B & H Publishing Group, 2013), 1.

[2] Mainline Protestants, including groups like the United Church of Christ, the Presbyterian Church (USA), the Episcopal Church, the United Methodist Church, and the Evangelical Lutheran Church in America, tend to be theologically liberal and guided by social justice ethics. Progressive Evangelicals,

repent and believe the gospel. But here comes the rub. If we ask ourselves whether our repentance is sincere, we look to an inner compass to give us a thumbs up or down on that score. But can we trust our inner compass to determine if we're truly repentant? Many of us suspect that our inner compass could deceive us. It might set too low a benchmark as the standard, and God, who doesn't slack from his standards, presumably, sets the highest standard possible. No wonder many Christians doubt their salvation! They can't let their guard down! Sorrow for sin is at the core of repentance. But, as noted, are you sorry enough? Even more, without repentance, there is no genuine faith in Christ.

More can be raised if those questions aren't enough to keep us busy. If faith is contingent on a decision for Christ, what becomes of my faith when I'm not conscious? After all, I spend about a third of my life sleeping. What happens to my faith when I'm asleep? It wouldn't seem that my faith is conscious while I'm sleeping, even if that slumber is a repository of dreams. What happens to my faith if I'm anesthetized for an operation? Does it disappear? Surely, under anesthesia, my faith isn't conscious. Or, what if I fall victim to dementia or a similar disease? Does my faith simply evaporate as my cognitive abilities dissipate? If so, faith would not seem to be a good means by which God saves us.

Ask yourself, though, where the onus for salvation is in this reasoning. Is it on Christ or ourselves? Clearly, the onus is on us. Yes, Jesus made it *possible* for us to

---

found within more doctrinally conservative groups such as the Southern Baptist Convention, advocate for social justice ethics, not so dissimilar from Mainline Protestants.

be saved. He died for our sins on the cross. But we're obliged to repent of our sins and decide for Jesus if we're going to benefit from his saving work. On the face of things, there are some problems with this logic. Such thinking comes across like a trade. We exchange our obedience in return for salvation. Is that the way we deal with God? Is God akin to a shady marketplace vendor? We need to put this way of thinking to the test. Is salvation really about trading our repentance for salvation from Christ? Do the scriptures teach this?

Further, must we be unrelentingly vigilant about the sincerity of our repentance? And, if that's true, is it because our sincerity saves us? If so, then why Jesus? If the onus is all on us, why did Jesus need to suffer for our sin? Maybe the advocates of deciding for Jesus, "decision theologians," will reframe the matter and contend that even though Jesus saves, our sincerity validates our decision for Jesus.

In seeking answers to these questions, we will look to the scriptures. We will also look to the thinking of the reformer Martin Luther. He, too, struggled over the question of his salvation, and he found the scriptures as an anchor for his assurance. His work shows us that the scriptures have a much broader approach to faith than reflective or cognitive awareness. Instead, faith is receptivity to God's Word, allowing God's Word to define your life at whatever point or stage in life you may be.

The New Birth as Passive

The worries about repentance expressed above need to be challenged. God isn't dependent on human consciousness to save us. He works in us even if we are unconscious or if our consciousness is not fully developed. For instance, when Mary visited Elizabeth prior to both John's and Jesus's birth, John the Baptist "leaped" in his mother Elizabeth's womb (Luke 1:41), a reaction to Mary's greeting Elizabeth. Elizabeth told Mary, "When the sound of your greeting came to my ears, the baby in my womb leaped for joy" (Luke 1:44). But, in the womb, John wasn't conscious like an adult is conscious. If that is the case, faith is a much bigger matter than consciousness. Even fetuses can exercise faith despite their undeveloped cognitive capacities! God works with the *whole person* throughout their lifespan, in all its stages of cognitive development and, presumably, mental demise. Hence, faith cannot be reduced to conscious awareness, let alone a decision. It is far too encompassing. It incorporates the believer's life in all its phases and manifestations. Ultimately, faith is human receptivity to God. It is the work of the Holy Spirit to plant Christ smack dab within our core and orient our entire life to Christ. Surprisingly, children have an advantage over adults concerning such receptivity. Jesus makes it clear that repentance doesn't entail that children need to become like adults but just the opposite: "Truly, I say to you, unless you turn and become like children, you will never enter the kingdom of heaven" (Matt 18:3). Jesus does not use the standard of adult consciousness as the measure for repentance but instead the receptivity, and humility, of a child. Adults must become like children in God's kingdom, not vice versa.

Deciding for Jesus is a cognitive matter. But, as we noted with John the Baptist in the womb, much of human life, including our relationship to God, transcends cognitive awareness. If that is the case, we should raise some questions about the revivalist tactic of urging sinners to "decide for Jesus." Obviously, this practice has been widespread for a couple of centuries. But is the practice scriptural? Many take it for granted that it is. But we need to let the scriptures guide our thinking. Addressing the Pharisee Nicodemus, Jesus said, ". . . unless one is born again he cannot see the kingdom of God" (John 3:3). Jesus' metaphor for conversion as a rebirth doesn't square with deciding for Jesus. Why? The metaphor of birthing rules out decision-making. *No baby chooses to be born.* Instead, a baby is pushed out of the womb by the mother. Babies exercise *no willpower* for their birth. Instead, the womb, of its own accord, on its timeline, pushes the baby out.

For a baby, birth is passive, not active. No one gives birth to themselves. Jesus applies this truth to the new birth (regeneration). God gives new birth just like mothers give birth. God is active, and the sinner is passive. Indeed, the sinner can only be receptive with respect to God. This truth is reinforced by the Greek word *anōthen* used for the English word "again" in the original text. The English Standard Version notes that *anōthen* has more than one meaning. In addition to "again," it can also mean "from above; the Greek is purposely ambiguous and can mean both again and from above."[1] Rendered as "from above," *anōthen*'s focus is on God who gives birth and not merely the event of rebirth. What does this all amount to? If we want to be true to Jesus when we speak of a new birth, we need to rule out decision-making. To experience a new birth is not an activity on our part, something we do. Instead, it is a passive event. If someone is "born again," it is because *God* has so birthed them.

---

[1] The Holy Bible, English Standard Version (Wheaton, Illinois: Good News Publishers, 2001), 1070.

Sinners' Decision for Jesus: Crucify Him!

Now, some will scratch their heads over this. How can our new birth be passive if Scripture asks us to receive Christ? Surely, if Scripture invites us to receive Christ, we should urge people to accept Jesus, right? Accepting is something active, isn't it? Decision theologians often appeal to John 1:12-13: "but to all who did receive him who believed in his name, he gave the right to become children of God, who were born not of blood nor of the will of the flesh nor of the will of man, but of God." Notice that this passage, like Jesus' nighttime discourse with Nicodemus, is about birth, a passive experience. But this passage also shouts that the will has *no agency* in regeneration. It disabuses us of the illusion that our will is free. Sin not only darkens the intellect but also distorts the will. Instead of living in faith as receptive to God and his goodness, our wills are captivated by sin and, as such, are perverted. The reformer Martin Luther described this state of the will as being "curved into" itself (incurvation). The will is captivated by its desires and seeks to fulfill those desires. It requires perpetual navel-gazing. But, the crucial point is that the desires themselves are not chosen. They are just there, and they are what drive our wills. People think they are in the driver's seat of their lives, the "masters of their own fates" or "captains of their own souls," as the poet William Ernest Henley put it, but they aren't. Instead, they are possessed by various desires, some of which conflict with each other, and these guide people in their decision-making. No neutral, desire-free pilot controls your life behind your eyeballs. Whatever you think of as your "self," it is possessed by desire. As sinners, these desires are invariably idolatrous, invested in a purported deity, or indifferent to God.

Jesus says the new birth is no exercise of the "will of the flesh nor of the will of man," but instead is due solely to God. If we are reborn, it is not because we exercise "free will," but the opposite. God gives us a new birth despite, even in opposition to, our will. In other words, receiving Christ happens not through any decision sinners make but only through the agency of the Holy Spirit, who brings them to faith. The Holy Spirit re-captivates us, like filling new vessels with new wine. We can never claim our reception of Christ as some performance *we* achieve. Instead, all the glory must be given to God. The reformer Martin Luther expressed this truth beautifully when, in his Small Catechism, he described the Spirit's regenerative agency:

> I believe that by my own understanding or strength I cannot believe in Jesus Christ my LORD or come to him, but instead the Holy Spirit has called me through the gospel, enlightened me with his gifts, made me holy and kept me in the true faith, just as he calls, gathers,

enlightens, and makes holy the whole Christian church on earth. . .[1]

Note well that John the Evangelist tells us that as believers, we have a *right* to claim our identity as God's children. Surely, this truth ought to help secure those Christians who doubt their salvation! Our *right* to claim our identity as God's children is grounded in the work of the Holy Spirit to bring about our new birth. A right is a claim, something due to a recipient. It is not based on the recipient's feelings or decisions. In this case, it is based on God's saving action. Our new birth is entirely in God's care. The onus is off us and should never have been put on us.

When Jesus invites "all who labor and are heavy laden" to come to him for rest (Matt 11:28), the weary only come because the Holy Spirit has compelled them to it. They lack the resources to provide rest in and of themselves. That is why Jesus delivers it for them. Likewise, all who respond to the "Spirit's and the Bride's" invitation to "come," which we read in Revelation 22:17, do so because the Spirit prompts, motivates, or impels them to do so. The Spirit motivates this response smack dab in the invitation as it is given. It is not necessarily the case that the call is irresistible. Old beings, or old Adams and Eves, guided by that aspect within us that is self-justifying, indifferent towards God and neighbors' needs, will always resist God's grace because they are so convinced that they don't need it. But, as God's accusing law breaks down sinners' self-confidence, it affords

---

[1] The Small Catechism in *The Book of Concord*, ed. Robert Kolb and Timothy J. Wengert (Minneapolis: Fortress, 2000), 355:6.

them no other avenue than God's mercy. When preachers repeat these scriptural invitations for people to come to Christ, they should not rhetorically package this bidding as an autonomous decision on the sinners' part. If someone comes to Christ, it is due solely to the work of the Spirit. "Decision theology" doesn't square with the new birth as an *entirely passive* experience. Concerning the language of decision, one of my seminary professors claimed, "Sure, you've made a decision for Jesus. As a sinner, your decision is to crucify him!" No doubt, that statement is off-putting. But isn't it accurate?

To put the matter in perspective, throughout most of Christianity's long history, believers have not described salvation in terms of deciding for Christ. That specific way of speaking is a strategy of the nineteenth-century revivalist Charles Finney, who assessed various methods by which speakers could sway their audience and motivate people to do what the speaker wanted. Given that the USA was a young democracy in the era he preached, he drew an analogy between the practice of voting for a president in the general election and sinners "voting" for God when they decide for Christ at a revival meeting. No doubt, as a democratic privilege, voting is empowering. Similarly, people are empowered as they vote for Jesus. But there are numerous problems with this analogy. First, God isn't like a president. To liken God to a president whom we elect is far too anthropomorphic a way of speaking about God. It dishonors God's deity. God is no one for whom you can vote. God is not just a grander divine version of ourselves.

In contrast, God is the one in whom we live, move, and have our being (Acts 17:28). God is the creator who continuously upholds all things in being. That means that we and all other creatures are completely dependent on God. Since God holds our destiny in his hands (and not vice versa), fear and trust, rather than decision-making, are the healthy responses that humans should have for God.

Secondly, the analogy between conversion and voting breaks down. Those facing death and hell don't feel that when Christ reaches out to them, they are somehow deciding for God, akin to deciding for one lukewarm dish over another in a buffet line. Those facing hell are desperate for rescue. They realize that they have no other option than Christ since he, having conquered death and hell, is Lord over them. To call this a "choice" is to caricature it. The human plight of facing hell is too desperate. No one can be saved unless the Holy Spirit draws them to Christ. Scripturally speaking, there is no purpose for someone to "decide" for Jesus even one time, let alone 5,000 times. Decision theology is wholly misguided. It undermines gospel-centered preaching, which, instead of asking something out of repentant sinners, actually delivers God's generous mercy by forgiving sin outright. As God's ambassadors, preachers proclaim God's forgiveness grounded in Christ's atoning work. Sinners need to claim this freely given forgiveness as their own. Preachers dare to give Christ to those within earshot.

The Free Will Illusion

Undoubtedly, "free will" is as American as apple pie. If there is one value that all Americans affirm, it is freedom. Americans assume that to be free is to exercise their will. (They seem to x-out the view that freedom is also liberation, such as liberation from sin, death, and the devil.) We can decide what to wear or what political party to align with. But, with respect to God, there is no such thing as free will. As mentioned above, God is not like a president, nor is faith at home in a buffet line of spiritual options. Instead, God provides even better *gifts* for our ongoing existence. To claim otherwise is an illusion, a fantasy.

Regarding ultimate matters, people are captivated by something or someone that they find desirable and life-affirming. That means that the will conforms to what it desires. And desires are not chosen. Similar to a romantic crush, they are, instead, suffered. Whatever you choose, you choose it to achieve your desire. No one forces you to choose anything regarding your perception of your ultimate good, to what's most important to you. But you find that those things that grab your heart are not things that you choose. Instead, strange as it sounds, they choose you. Stranger still, they possess you.

Describing how Martin Luther wrestled with his religious contemporaries who advocated that you could choose to live a better life and so earn God's grace, Professor Ken Sundet Jones shows the spiritual mischief that belief in "free will" brings. Many of Luther's religious contemporaries claimed that we could choose to love God if we tried hard enough. In so doing, we earn some merit with God, sufficient for God to grant us his grace. On the face of things, that medieval belief may come across as different from today's revivalists. But, to the degree that revivalism hooks into some exercise of the will, advancing human agency with respect to God, the two perspectives, medieval works-righteousness, and contemporary "born-againism," are similar. Jones writes:

> It all hinges on the assumption that you have free will. The Scholastic theology Luther was taught said that you have a spark of goodness left in your fallen, sinful self. The only thing needed is a little oomph from God's grace to fan it into flame. Then, you could exert your free will and decide to become the person God made you to be. You could freely opt for God's will, fulfill God's commands, and merit what Christ had done on the cross. The catchphrase of the theology was *facere quod in se est*, or "do what is within you to do." Choose to do your best, and God will do the rest. There were plenty of options for what you could choose: pilgrimages, visiting relics, entering a monastery, or donating cash to the church's latest fundraiser. The problem for Luther was that the focus remains on you; it all devolves into some moral system where God becomes a divine CPA, and Jesus is left out of the equation.[1]

---

[1] Ken Sundet Jones, *A Lutheran Toolkit* (Irvine, CA: New Reformation Publications, 2021), 18.

Evangelicals might not take much stock in pilgrimages or fasting. But they might invest a lot of their emotional energy in sexual chastity symbolized by a purity ring. No doubt, on the face of things, sexual purity is a good thing. It is worth maintaining. But, if it is ever used to justify oneself before God, some kind of "add-on" to Jesus, then it is misused. To be sure, purity culture is only one of many ways Christians seek to "add-on" to Jesus and his completed work. Likewise, any purity used to look down upon the impure is misused. Christ alone, not our behavior, is our purity through and through.

Flawed Logic

To summarize our findings so far, the "add-on" Christians operate with a logic of assurance that runs like this:

1. Anyone who accepts Jesus as Savior is saved.
2. I've accepted Jesus as Savior.
3. Therefore, I'm saved.

We have already noted that the major premise (#1) doesn't square with the passivity of rebirth. The minor premise (#2) leads to a host of hang-ups: Was I sincere? Did I accept Jesus wholeheartedly? Do I continue to accept Jesus, or have I slipped up? Was my repentance adequate? And the questions keep mounting. By inserting human effort into the equation about salvation, the "add-on" Christians undermine assurance, thus shifting the onus away from Christ and onto us.

Their approach is flawed. It assumes that you have free will and can choose to accept Jesus. But we have already seen how Jesus denies that the new birth is due to human willpower. We have also seen how the metaphor of birth is incompatible with choice. No one chooses to be born. Likewise, no sinner chooses a new birth. The "logic" above feeds the illusion that human sinfulness merely makes a dent in the human will rather than corrupting it entirely. But Paul thoroughly disagrees. Paul writes that we sinners "were dead in the trespasses and sins in which [we] once walked" (Eph 2:1). As dead sinners, our will has no agency to decide for Jesus. (Have you ever encountered a dead person making a choice?) If we are to be given new life, God must work a miracle! "But God, being rich in mercy, because of the great love with which he loved us, even when we were dead in our trespasses, made us alive together with Christ—by grace you have been saved—and raised us up with him and seated us with him in the heavenly places in Christ Jesus . . ." (Eph 2:4-6).

The Checklist

For some Christians, even a decision for Christ isn't enough. They fear a slacker approach to faith in which someone can accept Jesus as the Savior, but both fail to own him as Lord and abandon moral rectitude. In their view, repentance without allegiance to Christ's lordship doesn't cut it. After all, they reason that salvation involves not just God's acquittal of sinners for Jesus' sake but also a change of our natures, resulting in changed behaviors, dispositions, and traits. If I want to know that I'm saved, I need to check whether my behavior conforms to such godly living. For instance, John MacArthur, a leading Evangelical pastor and theologian, provides a checklist to help provide assurance of their salvation or lack thereof. If we progress in these matters, we (likely) are saved.[1] What's on the list? He provides eleven questions designed for our self-examination:

- Have you enjoyed fellowship with Christ and the Father?
- Are you sensitive to sin?

---

[1] John MacArthur, *Saved without a Doubt: Being Sure of Your Salvation* (Colorado Springs, CO: David Cook, 2011), 77-106.

- Do you obey God's Word?
- Do you reject this evil world?
- Do you eagerly await Christ's return?
- Do you see a decreasing pattern of sin in your life?
- Do you love other Christians?
- Do you experience answered prayer?
- Do you experience the ministry of the Holy Spirit?
- Can you discern between spiritual truth and error?
- Have you suffered rejection because of your faith?

MacArthur is convinced that the ability to answer these eleven questions in the affirmative confirms that someone is truly saved. Notice, too, that the focus is on you—what you should do or experience, not on God and what God must do for you and with you.

MacArthur is sure that these tests are biblical. No doubt, these standards are to be found in the scriptures. But as we have noted, MacArthur's focus is off. He sees these matters as something we do, as opposed to something God is working in us. Each question focuses on us and what we do to advance our spiritual life. He seems oblivious to the truth that ". . . we are his [God's] workmanship, created in Christ Jesus for good works, which God prepared beforehand, that we should walk in them" (Eph 2:10). It is not only that the Spirit brings us to faith, but the Spirit keeps us and advances us in the faith.

No doubt, in our Christian walk, we should examine ourselves in light of God's law, particularly the Ten Commandments, alongside the matters MacArthur raises. MacArthur likely thinks that, after examining themselves, truly saved individuals will discover just how much progress they have made in their Christian walk. But does that square with the child-like humility that Jesus points to? Isn't it more likely that Christians will see just how little they have advanced in their Christian lives and how much they need Jesus? We should treasure and foster spiritual practices such as prayer, devotional reading, and scriptural meditation. Such activities anchor us in God's Word so that God's Word permeates our thoughts and feelings. God's Word can pervade our imaginations and lead us to become more like Christ daily. These activities also accord with our nature since they remind us that, as creatures, we are completely dependent on God's mercy. But they are not to be used as steppingstones to secure or increase spiritual purity before God. Being clothed in Christ's righteousness is both necessary and sufficient for our standing before God (Zech 3:4).

Paul admonishes believers to examine themselves, particularly as they prepare to receive Holy Communion (1 Cor 11:28). But, in contrast to MacArthur, if done honestly, self-examination in light of God's law will show us how much we need Jesus. As noted, our motives are often not pure.

Often, we indeed are like servants terrified of God's punishment or toadies drooling for a heavenly reward. Either way, the old Adam or Eve is obsessed with "what's in it for me?" Despite that old, sinful person, God continually works to purify us. God's work upon us isn't always pleasant and is sometimes painful. That is because God has so much to tear down or hammer away at since we are bound to be curved in on ourselves. He's at work to break down our tendency to operate as either enslaved people or hirelings. His law judges and accuses us of our sinfulness. It proves to us our inability to pull ourselves up by our bootstraps. Far from being achievable for sinners, the law proves to be unachievable, and it unrelentingly accuses us old Adams and Eves.

God breaks down the illusion that our behavior as either servants or hirelings helps us avoid hell or gain heaven. He does this just so that he can create within us pure, clean hearts (Ps 51:10). He does this by allowing these illusions to work themselves out in our lives, bringing us to their dead end.

No doubt, it isn't easy to read that God pains us in order to disestablish our old sinful self. Martin Luther described this breaking down of illusions as an "alien work" and distinguished it from God's "proper work," which is comfort. God's alien work is like how a surgeon must make incisions to operate on a sick person, allowing infection to drain or cancer to be excised. In God's alien work, we learn that life is not, as Frank Sinatra put it, doing things "my way." That kind of narcissism proves, in the long run, to be an empty sham. God is about making *new* creations (2 Corinthians 5:17). Professor Wade Johnston says it beautifully:

> The Spirit is not in this [new birth] for a quick buck. He does not come in and flip a house. No, He renews it and makes it His temple and eternal dwelling place. This renovation is not a matter of some paint and new floors. The Holy Spirit kills and makes alive, drowns and raises.[2]

---

[2] Wade Johnston, *An Uncompromising Gospel: Lutheranism's First Identity Crisis and Lessons for Today* (Irvine, CA: New Reformation Publications, 2016), 83.

Nor should we cling to the illusion, as many sinners do, that we should be like Atlas shouldering the entire world. Many deceive themselves into thinking that apart from themselves, especially with their help for others, everything would collapse. That's a lot of pressure to live with! But lots of people attempt it and suffer the consequences of doing so! God allows our illusions to lead us to a dead end precisely so that we find no other resource than his mercy, granted in Christ, to rescue us. He saves us from ourselves—our own out-of-sync ways of managing our lives. Whatever script we adopt as sinners always amounts to the same self-focus and incurvation. MacArthur wants to shift the burden of our Christian life back onto us. But isn't that tantamount to more incurvation, albeit in a pious guise? It is not our decisions or religious affections,[3] important as those are, or even renewed moral dispositions, that prove that we are justified or regenerate. Christ's promise alone justifies us and gives us a new birth. Christ alone is our defense concerning our sinfulness and even against those good things we use to vindicate ourselves. To be sure, this is not said to spite doing good. Far from it! But it is said to call out self-righteousness.

Unless one has a low benchmark for sinlessness, only a Pharisee can answer MacArthur's questions in the affirmative. Because we sin not only in our behaviors but also in the smallest of our thoughts and deeds, no one, on a daily basis, in complete honesty, can say that they score "excellent," let alone "good" or "average" for

---

[3] John Piper, *What Is Saving Faith? Reflections on Receiving Christ as a Treasure* (Wheaton, Illinois: Crossway, 2022), 11-13.

each of these categories. Christians will always struggle with their old natures, which remain opposed to God and his ways. Our old nature always believes that it can do a much better job being God than God could. This rascal can't be reformed. It can only be put to death, and that on a daily basis.

MacArthur sets high standards for the Christian life. Some may be attracted to his way of thinking for this reason. Many Americans set high standards and believe that hustle makes the difference. Of course, we should not tolerate slacking in our jobs, schoolwork, or extra-curricular activities. With MacArthur, they may feel that perfectionism operating in their daily lives can be transferred into their faith walk. Whoever can improve their skills in their faith journey can also perfect them. Anyone doing better can do their best if they try hard enough. Many put tons of pressure on themselves to perform. Not a few of them suffer anxiety and depression for this reason.

For MacArthur, you cannot claim the benefits of Christ as Savior if you fail to give your allegiance to him as Lord. Each item on the checklist is designed to help you show your allegiance to Christ's kingship. But, this approach fails to see that Christ establishes his lordship over this rebellious creation (Matt 12:29; Col 1:13), including ourselves. As a good Lord, Christ reaches out to rescue the lost, those at enmity with him. Paul wrote, ". . . but God shows his love for us in that while we were still sinners, Christ died for us . . . For if while we were *enemies* we were reconciled to God by the death of his Son, much more, now that we are reconciled, shall we be saved by his life" (Rom 5:8, 10, italics mine). The overall scriptural direction between

God and sinners is that of God reaching out to sinners to deliver them, not sinners proving their worth to God. It isn't as if God doesn't have expectations of believers. He does. Paul offers powerful exhortations in his epistles (See Romans 12-15 for one example). But nowhere does the follow-through on such tasks grant assurance of salvation. Christ *alone* is the assurance of our salvation.

I feel for those with anxious consciences, fearing God's wrath, to learn from MacArthur. He argues that if you want assurance of salvation, you must follow a checklist of add-ons to Jesus, including willingness to be martyred, answered prayer, obedience, etc. Some matters to which he appeals are not in believers' control. Either way, those with anxious consciences are going to become more anxious. Of those matters over which we exercise some control, such as our rejection of the evil world, the disturbing question arises: "Have I rejected it enough, or could I reject it even more?" If we look to our resources alone, there is no let up on the pedal. We will be hounded to death forever. Of those matters over which we have no control, such as whether or not our prayers are answered, we cannot help but be anxious as well. After all, we have no say in whether or not our prayers are answered. The standards don't disappear. The standards are good and wholesome. But, in Christ, the accusations disappear (Rom 8:1).

Does our salvation then come down to "Jesus plus"? Jesus + answered prayer? Jesus + obedience? Undoubtedly, MacArthur wants to give us a view of faith where no one can or should slack off. But he seems unable to comprehend a soul tormented by the

accusations of God's law. Perhaps if he took his checklist to heart, he too would experience such torment
from the law's attack. For those focused on making
decisions for Jesus or tallying points on a checklist,
we are guided to look to *ourselves* to see whether or
not we are saved. We need to trust in a decision we've
made or whether we can muster evidence or feelings
to show that we have experienced a change of heart.
To confess as the possessed boy's father did to Jesus, "I
believe; help my unbelief!" (Mark 9:24) is too mediocre
a stance. Yet all Christians wrestle with such unbelief.
We daily contend with our old nature. Sin, after all, is
not merely being naughty. It is a person's entire disposition or orientation—being turned in on the self and
away from God—a perversion of the heart. The heart
was designed to honor God above all things and love
others for their own sake, but sinners think that they
can do a better job than God at being god for themselves. No wonder that a whole new birth is required
to be saved!

The above critique is not offered to challenge the
reality of new life in Christ. Paul reveled in this new life.
Luther, too, praised it. The reformer described it thus:

> Thus a new creation is a work of the Holy Spirit, who
> implants a new intellect and will and confers the power
> to curb the flesh and to flee the righteousness and wis-
> dom of the world. This is not a sham or merely a new
> outward appearance, but something really happens. A
> new attitude and a new judgment, namely, a spiritual
> one, actually come into being, and they now detest what
> they once admired. Our minds were once so captivated
> by the monastic life that we thought of it as the only

way to salvation; now we think of it quite differently. What we used to adore, before this new creation, as the ultimate in holiness now makes us blush when we remember it.[4]

Notice here that the new creation with its new affections and will is not presented as something we can conjure. Instead, it is something that the Holy Spirit creates in us as God's Word permeates into our souls.

---

[4] Lectures on Galatians (1535), in *Luther's Works* (St. Louis: Concordia, 1964), vol. 27:140-41.

Christ Alone

If we are going to be true to Paul, we need to ask, what if the assurance of salvation doesn't come down to looking for something within ourselves to confirm it? What if assurance of salvation wholly depended on Christ, completely separate from our feelings, decisions, or behaviors? This question isn't asked to devalue our emotions, decisions, and behavior but instead ground the basis of the assurance of our salvation.

On the face of things, it makes sense that assurance of salvation would wholly depend upon Christ since our salvation is due solely to Christ's atoning work. In addition to the scriptures, important early Christian thinkers were in tune with the truth that the assurance of our salvation rests in Jesus Christ alone. For instance, the anonymous author of the Epistle to Diognetus (second century AD) wrote:

> But when our unrighteousness was fulfilled, and it had been made perfectly clear that its wages—punishment and death—were to be expected, then the season arrived, during which God had decided to reveal at last his goodness and power (oh, the surpassing kindness and love of God!). He did not hate us, or reject us, or bear a grudge against us; instead, he was patient and

forbearing; in his mercy, he took upon himself our sins; he himself gave up his own Son as a ransom for us, the holy one for the lawless, the guiltless for the guilty, "the just for the unjust," the incorruptible for the corruptible, the immortal for the mortal. For what else but his righteousness could have covered our sins? In whom was it possible for us, the lawless and ungodly, to be justified, except in the Son of God alone? O the sweet exchange, O the incomprehensible work of God, O the unexpected blessings, that the sinfulness of many should be hidden in one righteous man, while the righteousness of one should justify many sinners![1]

This ancient author is a true gospel preacher! He lifts the burden of salvation from our shoulders. True enough, he understands that God holds us accountable for sin. But that said, we are completely unable to un-incurvate ourselves. We cannot change the condition of our hearts as disordered, curved in upon themselves. Only God can bring about a new creation and give sinners a new status before him: children, as opposed to either servants or hirelings and give them new, clean hearts. The author does not have us look to our behavior, feelings, or decisions to affirm our salvation. Instead, he draws our attention to Christ alone. Christ is not only necessary to save us from sin, death, and the devil, but he is also sufficient. *Jesus Christ is enough*. There is nothing in ourselves that must be added-on to Jesus.

Indeed, to add *anything* to the cross is to insult our Lord. His agonizing death and his glorious resurrection

---

[1] Thomas Schreiner, *Faith Alone: The Doctrine of Justification* (Grand Rapids: Zondervan, 2015), 29.

are enough. We should not look at ourselves and judge if our inner state or outward behavior matches some checklist. Instead, we are to look *outside* ourselves to Christ. Better said, we are to listen to Christ and the promises he makes us. *Our faith is never in our faith.* Our faith is always outside us, resting in Christ, trusting in his promises.

What are those promises? Here are some you shouldn't miss.

- 1 John 1:8-9: "If we say we have no sin, we deceive ourselves, and the truth is not in us. If we confess our sins, he is faithful and just to forgive us our sins and to cleanse us from all unrighteousness."
- Ephesians 1:7-8: "In him [Christ] we have redemption through his blood, the forgiveness of our trespasses, according to the riches of his grace, which he lavished upon us, in all wisdom and insight making known to us the mystery of his will. . . "
- Isaiah 43:25: "I, I am he who blots out your transgressions for my own sake, and I will not remember your sins."
- Psalm 103:12: ". . . as far as the east is from the west, so far does he remove our transgression from us."
- Psalm 32:1: "Blessed is the one whose transgression is forgiven, whose sin is covered."
- Romans 8:1: "There is therefore now no condemnation for those who are in Christ Jesus."

God doesn't merely overlook our sins. He takes them on in Jesus Christ, specifically in Jesus' death. The great medieval theologian Bernard of Clairvaux emphasized that because Jesus was our substitute and took on all our sins, he has a twofold right to heaven. Luther loved this imagery as well.[2] Christ's first right to heaven is because he is God and, as God, has a right to heaven. His second right is grounded in the fact that Christ fulfilled God's law and paid the penalty for sin on the cross. He can give this right to whomever he chooses (John 1:12). God's heart is merciful. And God wants to claim sinners as his own. Jesus says, "I have not come to call the righteous but sinners to repentance" (Luke 5:32), which means Christ ultimately has a place for you in his heavenly mansion and right now as his disciple, no matter how imperfect you may be. Christ shares his right to a place next to God in heaven with you (Isa 57:15).

The fact that assurance of salvation is grounded in Christ alone, just like salvation itself is grounded in Christ alone, doesn't mean Christians should slack from doing good. Instead, it allows those works to be truly good since we would no longer be doing them to secure the assurance of our salvation. In other words, we would avoid ulterior motives. We wouldn't be doing good works to prove something about our status with God and use them to leapfrog over others in their need. We could care about people in need and not merely see our doing good to them as a transaction between ourselves and God.

An important way that Christians have addressed the question of human salvation is through the doctrine of justification by grace alone through faith alone. God's grace or mercy, his "favor," awakens faith in those

---

[2] Sermons on the Gospel of John (1537-40), in *Luther's Works* (St. Louis: Concordia, 1957), vol. 22:269.

whom the Spirit pleases so that they grasp Jesus Christ and thereby are saved from sin, death, and the devil. No longer does the law's accusations of your sin have any merit when Jesus Christ is your defender and advocate. Christ covers you in his righteousness, and the accusation of the law no longer has any weight or merit. Christ is your defender; you are secure.

Justification by Grace Alone

Now, to speak of Christ's righteousness as given or "imputed" to sinners is to address the doctrine of justification. Protestants say that sinners are justified by grace alone through faith alone. Not everyone is on board with that view. In this understanding, justification is seen as "forensic": God granting his favor to sinners, declaring them forgiven, for Jesus' sake. The word "forensic" arose from the public forum in antiquity, where public debate led to pronouncing formal judgments and involved a twofold meaning: to give a verdict of righteousness and speak authoritatively. God's verdict to forgive sinners, for Jesus' sake, provides them a new status where they can no longer be legitimately attacked by the law. Nothing is surer since it is God who authorizes this judgment.

For some thinkers, such as Augustine, justification is understood as "transformative," sinners becoming righteous based on their renewal in Christ. For Augustine, the transformative view is the only workable approach to justification.[1] It's not Christ's righteousness as accounted to believers for Jesus' sake that justifies,

---

[1] Thomas Schreiner, *Faith Alone: The Doctrine of Sanctification* (Grand Rapids: Zondervan, 2015): 34.

but instead, believers are made righteous over time. No doubt grace initiates the process that leads believers to eternal life and sustains them. But, in the transformative view, sinners can never be fully assured of their salvation until they are completely perfected, which will happen only in the afterlife. Following this perspective, Roman Catholics believe that those dying in venial sin, sin which does not separate you from God's grace, will suffer in purgatory and finally reach that perfection. While venial sin doesn't damn, it still needs to be purged from our system. Purgatory will inflict pain on sinners, similar to that of those suffering in hell, but such pain will bring about sinners' purification and so grant them access to heaven.

Martin Luther and other Protestant reformers in the sixteenth century disagreed with this approach to justification. They saw justification in forensic terms, which emphasized that, with respect to God, our *status*, and thus our actual identity, has been changed. God's way of seeing or regarding things makes things become what they are. Christ's righteousness based on his atoning work is mercifully given to sinners. *His* righteousness is accounted as *their* own. This gift is no legal fiction since Christ can give his righteousness to whomever he chooses. Likewise, sinners ultimately have nothing to offer God other than their faith. The reformers didn't deny that believers experience not just a change of status but also a change of *nature*, that is, that through faith, they become new creations in Christ (2 Corinthians 5:17). But they argued that the forensic approach took precedence over the transformative, that sinners' change of status as forgiven sinners served as the basis for their change of nature, their new birth, and not vice versa. Hence, for the reformers, there is an "effective" dimension to justification, in which believers' natures are indeed renewed. But it is grounded in and dependent on justification as forensic, the change of status from being a sinner to being a forgiven sinner.

The forensic approach to justification led Luther to affirm a paradox: Christians are simultaneously saints and sinners (*simul iustus et peccator*). Naturally, many Christians would deny this. In contrast, they would say that sinners are in the process of becoming saints. But Luther calls out this common perspective as a problem. He acknowledged that we are saints because Christ's righteousness has been imputed to us, Christ's blood covers our sins (1 John 1:7), and our status with God has been changed, even though our old nature remains sinful. The pastoral implication of this *simul* approach is that, with Christ's righteousness imputed to us, we are secure in Christ. Even though our thoughts, feelings, and desires are imperfect, we need not doubt our salvation. Once this understanding of righteousness had been handed over to me through genuine gospel preaching in my later teenage years, I could rest secure in Christ. No doubt, MacArthur and company would be distressed by this. To him, Luther's approach guarantees that we'll all remain spiritual slackers, unworthy of God. But he's off-target. Luther affirms not merely forensic justification, but he also acknowledges that it is effective. Our security in Christ has implications for our lives. God is in the business of making new creatures with new desires and behaviors, even if that newness is not the basis for the assurance of salvation. As Paul writes, ". . . he [God] who began a good work in you will bring it to completion at the day of Jesus Christ" (Phil 1:6). Trust in Christ's forgiving words includes the trust that we are now righteous and thus we want to live like Christ and serve our neighbors.

As mentioned, saving faith is neither faith in our own faith nor in our decisions, feelings, or thoughts. Instead, faith's object lies outside of ourselves, in Christ. As Paul put it, faith comes by hearing and hearing by the Word of God (Rom 10:17). (Ears are the most passive of all our body's organs.) The Word promises that we are not only accounted righteous for Jesus' sake since he bore our sins, but God also wants to make us new creations. That means that faith receives Christ as God's favor toward us and Christ as already dwelling within us, within our hearts (Eph 3:17), establishing us as new creations. Through the Holy Spirit, Christ dwells within us. Again, that is not an invitation for us to assess our inner state and determine just how much of Christ is within us, how much of our being is controlled by Christ, or any other such analysis that breeds a lack of assurance. But it is a way of recognizing that we are new people in Christ. As Paul put it, "I have been crucified with Christ. It is no longer I who live, but *Christ who lives in me.* And the life I now live in the flesh I live by faith in the Son of God, who loved me and gave himself for me" (Gal 2:20, italics mine). There is an effective dimension to justification in which God is working to dismantle the power of the old Adam within us and establish Christ in our hearts through faith.[2] By faith, we

---

[2] For an elaboration, see "Apostles' Creed, Article III," introduced and annotated by Mark Mattes in *Luther's Large Catechism with Annotations and Contemporary Applications*, ed. John T. Pless and Larry M. Vogel (St. Louis: Concordia 2022), 403-422.

can affirm that we make some progress in this matter. Martin Luther described it beautifully:

> For this life is a constant progress from faith to faith, from love to love, from patience to patience, and from affliction to affliction. It is not righteousness, but justification; not purity, but purification; we have not yet arrived at our destination, but we are all on the road, and some are farther advanced than others. God is satisfied to find us busy at work and full of determination. When he is ready he will come quickly, strengthen faith and love, and in an instant take us from this life to heaven. But while we live on earth we must bear with one another, as Christ also bore with us, seeing that none of us is perfect.[3]

Such transformation is premised on our salvation, which is grounded in Christ's righteousness being imputed to us. It includes our daily resistance to the old nature, our struggle to "put off" the old self, and to "put on the new self, created after the likeness of God in true righteousness and holiness" (Eph 4:22, 24). It can be described as an ongoing, continuous conversion, always bringing the gifts of our new birth each day.

Luther and other thinkers, following the scriptures, regard this forensic justification as based on a "joyous exchange." Christ assumes—takes on—our sins, and he dresses us in his own righteousness. Paul even went so far as to say that Christ became sin on our behalf (2 Cor 5:21). This doesn't mean Jesus ever sinned. That

---

[3] Confession and the Lord's Supper in *The Complete Sermons of Martin Luther*, trans. John Nicholas Lenker, vol. 1.2 (Grand Rapids: Baker, 2000), 212.

can't be the case, or he would need a Savior. But he is the Lamb of God who takes away the sin of the world (John 1:29) precisely because, like the lambs sacrificed under the Old Covenant rituals, he bears sin. When he died on the cross, any accusation against us from God's law that we are sinners died with him (Col 2:14). Jesus is your defender even when your guard is down, when you are asleep, or unconscious, even in the face of whatever poor decisions your future self will make. Jesus has you covered. Faith grasps Christ. But what we discover is that it is Christ who is holding, carrying, and grasping us. As people of faith, we look to nothing in ourselves or of ourselves but to Christ alone. If we have a hard time believing that Jesus really forgives our sins, we should avail ourselves of private confession and absolution. This is an opportunity to share our sins with the pastor, who, in the pastoral office, is the "ear of Christ." (All Christians are called to do this, but one should confess with a pastor if one is available.) The pastor will then absolve you of your sins. This absolution comes as the very words of Christ himself.[4] No checklist, including our decisions, feelings, or moral commitments, can compare with Christ's own words. Nothing is stronger than the Word of God.

---

[4] For more on confession and absolution see Matthew C. Harrison, "Holy Absolution," and Brent W. Kuhlman "Why Private Confession?" in *Luther's Large Catechism with Annotations and Contemporary Applications*, ed. John T. Pless and Larry M. Vogel, 703-711.

Once Saved, Always Saved?

The same Christians who tend to advance add-ons to Jesus, such as "Christ + my decision," "Christ + my affections," or "Christ + my obedience," also tend to affirm "once saved, always saved." We need to be very careful with such slogans. We all have met someone who, at thirteen years old, "got saved" at Bible camp but by the end of their sophomore year in college had become a committed atheist. Jesus tells us, "If anyone does not abide in me, he is thrown away like a branch and withers; and the branches are gathered, thrown into the fire, and burned" (John 15:6). In light of this warning, we must cling to Jesus' *promise*: "I give them [my sheep] eternal life, and they will never perish, and no one will snatch them out of my hand. My Father, who has given them to me, is greater than all, and no one is able to snatch them out of the Father's hand" (John 10:28-29). People can fall away from Jesus, and if they persist in their unbelief, they commit the sin against the Holy Spirit (Matt 12:31). The Holy Spirit works to draw us to Christ. If someone insists on resisting the Spirit, they jeopardize their salvation. With stern language, Hebrews warns:

> For it is impossible to restore again to repentance those who have once been enlightened, who have tasted

the heavenly gift, and have shared in the Holy Spirit, and have tasted the goodness of the word of God and the powers of the age to come, if they then fall away, since they are crucifying once again the Son of God to their own harm and holding him up to contempt (Heb 6:4-6).

(If you are worried that you have sinned against the Holy Spirit, you most certainly have not! Those who commit the sin against the Holy Spirit never worry about committing it. Trust the truth that Jesus rescues sinners, and that means you!) There is finally no explanation why some children run away from home and never return. Jesus makes it clear there's no point asking why some don't repent. In this life, we are not privy to why some come to faith, and others do not. That's God's business and not our business. But, if we are truly concerned for the lost, it behooves us to share God's promise to any who will listen and allow the Holy Spirit to do his work in them. While we don't know why some resist repentance, Jesus still calls all to repent (Luke 13:1-5) and believe the gospel (Mark 1:15).

God's warnings are never to be trifled with. But he does not always execute them. Jonah, for instance, was told to preach an unconditional judgment to the Ninevites. They were not afforded the opportunity to repent. "Yet forty days, and Nineveh shall be overthrown!" (Jonah 3:4). Now, the Ninevites *did* repent (even though they weren't offered this as an option), and Nineveh was spared. Likewise, Jesus preaches not to sin against the Spirit: "Not everyone who says to me, "Lord, Lord," will enter the kingdom of heaven, but the one who does the will of my Father who is in heaven"

(Matt 7:21). God's will, of course, is that we repent of sin and believe the gospel. Jesus offers this warning not to invalidate the gospel he has come to bring but to call out a false security in which people don't trust in him but instead in their works (Matt 7:22). Again, the bottom-line concerning believers' assurance of salvation is not add-ons but instead claiming God's promise of forgiveness. God is true to his Word. The "once saved, always saved" slogan fails to see that repentance is an ongoing process, something which God is continually working within us, in which day by day we see just how much more we need Jesus and his mercy. Conversion is a daily event in which we entrust our whole being to God's care.

An Antidote for Slacking?

A number of add-on or checklist Christians carp that a distinction between Christ as Savior and Christ as Lord should be made. From that distinction, they claim that those who refuse Christ as Lord cannot claim him as Savior. What's going on here? Again, this crowd is often terrified that the gospel might be presented as "cheap grace," which would allow believers to slack. The implication is that, in principle, someone could accept Jesus as their Savior but fail to meet the requirements to honor him as Lord. Real Christians will give their full allegiance to Christ as Lord and behave accordingly. But the view of Christ's lordship is a little haywire here. First off, grace is never cheap. It cost Jesus his life. It also costs sinners their lives! But let's also be honest: Christ is Lord because he is God (Matt 2:2; Ps 110:1f; 1 Cor 15:25). Human allegiance cannot alter the status of Christ's lordship. Christ is Lord regardless of how we behave. Repentance is a reality check on what I have been doing and who God is. Ideally, of course, a Christian should behave like Christ. Jesus is indeed not only our salvation; he is also the example of how we should live (Eph 5:1; Phil 2:3-8). What add-on Christians fail to reckon with is that Christ establishes his lordship over his rebellious creation in his own time and in his own way. He establishes his lordship in the church through preaching the law, which brings human incurvation to naught, and the gospel, which calls forth new beings in Christ. He works through governments to bring stability so families can raise children and contribute to human flourishing. So, matters are off with the "add-on" Christians. If Jesus is your Savior, he is your Lord. Your allegiance or lack thereof does not alter that fact. If your old Adam or Eve gains the upper hand in your life, Christ's lordship over you is not diminished. He remains Lord even if you do a poor job as his servant.

Paul, an advocate of justification by grace alone through faith alone, certainly was no slacker nor an advocate of slacking.

> But whatever gain I had, I counted as loss for the sake of Christ. Indeed, I count everything as loss because of the surpassing worth of knowing Christ Jesus my Lord. For his sake I have suffered the loss of all things and count them as rubbish, in order that I may gain Christ and be found in him, not having a righteousness of my own that comes from the law, but that which comes through faith in Christ, the righteousness from God that depends on faith—that I may know him and the power of his resurrection, and may share his suffering, becoming like him in his death, that by any means possible I may attain the resurrection from the dead (Phil 3:7-11).

Notice Paul's passion to "press on toward the goal of the prize of the upward call of God in Christ Jesus" (Phil 3:14) is grounded in the truth that he embraces a passive righteousness from Christ and not an active one based on doing the law's works. The apostle is confident that the gospel awakens believers to do good, make a difference in the world, and live as "little christs" in the world. Christians cannot save as Christ does, but they can help their neighbors in need. This motivating energy empowered by the gospel, which transforms believers, never detracts them from their need for Christ. Christ is the fount and source to which they daily return for sustenance. Believers strive to improve their skills (and strengths and health) to enhance their agency for doing good. But such striving is never about accruing brownie points with God. Again, as believers, Christians are no longer stooges of incurvation. Instead, over and over again, they return to Christ, find forgiveness in him, and renew themselves to face new (and even reappearing old) challenges from day to day.

For some, this description of the Christian life seems to endorse mediocrity. Surely, Christians should be living the best life possible, right? Surely Christian authors (like me) shouldn't advocate that Christians sell themselves short. Even the military once advertised its ability to help recruits "be all they can be." How would the Christian life be any different?

As noted earlier, Paul said that he had been crucified with Christ. At the heart of the Christian life is the cross. Unlike Jesus' cross, the cross we bear does not take away the world's sins. Thank God for that! But we undergo trial and opposition as we confess and live out our faith. We encounter attacks from the accuser that pain us because often they are valid. We have failed to do our best. But, we also experience disempowerment as we face resistance and opposition to the good we seek to establish in our homes, places of employment, and the wider community. All this opposition reinforces that our own resources are lacking. We need Christ to sustain us all along the way, for his resources are unlimited. He helps us see that the flipside of the crosses we daily experience is the resurrection. In other words, God's grace is also given to us daily. It continues to empower us so that we do not grow weary. It is never possible to remove the cross from the Christian life. Nor should we seek it to be since it is a crucial way God shapes us into people of faith.

The Paul who is in the cheer squad for Christ in Philippians 3 is the same Paul who in 2 Corinthians 12:1-10 reveals how God sent him a "thorn" in the flesh to humble him, to force him to rely on Christ, and not on his own power. God did this so that Paul would learn that when he is "weak" in himself, he can find strength in Christ (2 Cor 12:10). Such weakness doesn't make Paul a slacker. Nor does it indicate that he failed to give his all to Jesus as Lord. Instead, it shows us that we should never look to our own resources for living the Christian life. Not only is Christ necessary and sufficient to save, but he is also necessary and sufficient for us to live the Christian life. To hammer this point home, Paul appeals to baptism. "We were buried therefore with him [Christ] by baptism into death, in order that, just as Christ was raised from the dead by the glory of the Father, we too might walk in newness of life" (Rom 6:4). Indeed, "we know that our old self was crucified with him [Christ] in order that the body of sin might be brought to nothing, so that we would no longer be enslaved to sin . . . Now if we have died with Christ, we believe that we will also live with him" (Rom 6:6, 8). If we are to believe Paul, God has acted in baptism to bring the old being to naught and raise us anew. We can have assurance of our salvation because God has acted upon us in baptism.

If Paul is right that God works to claim you as a new person in Christ, you can be sure of your salvation. The burden of proving your sincerity in repentance isn't on you. Instead, the whole event of salvation is on God—no matter how imperfectly you repent. Chances are, you'll need to repent daily anyway. But the onus of salvation is all on God, not on you. God has given you a promise, and even if your faith is weak and tiny, like a mustard seed (Matt 17:20), God remains true to his Word. That Word is spoken in your baptism in which the Triune God, Father, Son, and Holy Spirit commits himself to you, promises to be your God, and takes care of you.

Baptism as a Means of Grace

Many Christians see baptism as merely a symbol of their decision to believe in Jesus. They don't see baptism as a means of grace. No doubt, they would find that idea off-putting. Surely baptism isn't some magic, is it? Just get baptized, and all will be fine, whether or not you believe. On top of that, many are baptized in infancy: how did they ever repent and believe? Surely, baptizing babies isn't what God wants.

There is a deeper matter in this discussion about baptism: what the Christian life is about. Is the Christian life largely a program we follow, or is it a declaration that Christ embraces us and gives himself to us for life and salvation? Those who deny baptism is efficacious—a means through which God works to transform us—are apt to follow the former position, while those who see baptism as efficacious are likely to follow the latter.

Again, we need to look to the scriptures. What do they say about baptism?

- Jesus clarifies that it is a means of making people become disciples (Matt 28:19). Baptism confers the gift of God's divine and saving name. All the gifts conferred in baptism flow from the gift of the divine and saving name of God.

- Jesus describes baptism as a means of regeneration (John 3:5). Paul likewise calls it a "washing of regeneration" (Titus 3:5).

- Peter tells his audience on the first Pentecost that baptism leads to the remission of sins (Acts 2:38). Not only is baptism for children (Acts 2:39), but it confers the gift of the Holy Spirit, who confirms the truth of our adoption as God's children.

- Paul tells us it "washes away sins" (Acts 22:16; Eph 5:25-26).

- Paul notes baptism unites us to Christ's death and resurrection in Romans 6, Galatians 3:27, and Colossians 2:12.

- And, if there were any other doubts, Peter says point blank that baptism saves (1 Pet 3:21). Baptism is not like washing dirt off externally. It goes to the heart of a person, to the conscience, which now stands clean before God because it has been raised with Christ in baptism. God saved Noah and his family through the water. That water typifies holy baptism, which saves you through Jesus's resurrection.

Baptism is not magic. But neither is it a mere symbol of our discipleship or loyalty to Christ. Instead, it is a means of grace, something God uses to deliver Jesus' benefits. Christ instituted it. It's not the water itself in baptism that saves, but it is water connected with Christ's promise and done in the name of the triune God who saves, just as Scripture teaches. Luther writes,

> Clearly the water does not do it, but the Word of God, which is with and alongside the water, and faith, which trusts this Word of God in the water. For without the

> Word of God, the water is plain water and not a bap-
> tism, but with the Word of God, it is a baptism, that
> is, a grace-filled water of life and a 'bath of the new
> birth in the Holy Spirit,' as St. Paul says to Titus in
> chapter 3. . . .[1]

Does that mean that you can trust your baptism for
salvation? In a word, yes. If baptism were our action, the
answer would be no. But baptism is God's work upon
sinners to claim them as his own and assure them that
they are his children. Of course, it is faith that trusts
God's promise of salvation given in baptism that allows
us to claim the mercy given in baptism for ourselves.
Baptism is no mere human ceremony, but a sacrament
established by Christ to deliver and secure your salvation. In this light, we can propose an alternative syllo-
gism to the one advocated by the add-on Christians. It
runs like this:

1. Christ assures us that all who are baptized are saved.
2. I have been baptized.
3. Therefore, I am saved.

Now, mind you, the benefits of baptism can be received
only in faith. If you don't trust in Christ's promise, you
can't anticipate that the mere performance of baptism
saves. That would indeed be magic. But by trusting
Christ's promise attached to the water and given in
baptism, your baptism saves you.

---

[1] The Small Catechism in *The Book of Concord*, ed. Robert
Kolb and Timothy J. Wengert, p. 359.

Infant Baptism

Some will object to infant baptism. They reason from the decision theology critiqued above that infants can't decide for Jesus, at least in any cognitive way. We noted earlier how Jesus tells us that it isn't infants who must become like adults to be fit candidates for salvation but just the opposite: adults must become like children (Matt 18:3). That said, we might want some further explanation about infant baptism given that we are a culture obsessed with validating our sense of self by exercising our freedom through decisions. As noted above, the Holy Spirit motivated John the Baptist, even in the womb, to rejoice in Christ. This rejoicing was no conscious decision on John's part. But it was a reaction of faith. Surely, if fetuses in utero can have faith, infants can too.

In orthodox systems of viewing faith, faith is seen as having three components: (1) knowledge, (2) assent, and (3) trust. Unlike teens and adults, knowledge and assent for infants are intuitive and not cognitive, but it is still faith. King David teaches that infants have faith: "Yet you are he who took me from the womb; you made me trust you at my mother's breasts. On you was I cast from my birth, and from my mother's womb you have been my God" (Ps 22:9-10). Likewise, Psalm 71:6 says,

"Upon you I have learned from before my birth; you are he who took me from my mother's womb." Likewise, Jesus teaches that little children (*paidia*) have faith, "but whoever causes one of these little ones who believe in me to sin, it would be better for him to have a great millstone fastened around his neck and to be drowned in the depth of the sea" (Matt 18:6). In Luke, Jesus is even more adamant about infant faith (*brephos*): "Let the children come to me, and do not hinder them, for to such belongs the kingdom of God. Truly, I say to you, whoever does not receive the kingdom of God like a child shall not enter it" (Luke 18:15-17). When children acclaimed Jesus as the Son of David, Jesus noted, referencing Psalm 8:2 from the Septuagint (the Greek translation of the Hebrew scriptures), that "Out of the mouth of infants and nursing babies you have prepared praise" (Matt 21:6). Indeed, a child's disposition doesn't have the defensiveness and resistance to God as does that of adults. Adults must become like little children if they are to receive Christ. Jesus welcomed children into his community of disciples (Matt 19:14; Mark 10:14-15). As welcomed by him, surely, they are fit candidates for baptism. When Jesus commanded his disciples to baptize, he never specified the exclusion of children. For that reason, Christians historically have offered baptism for infants and children. More to the point, children, too, are sinners and need salvation.

Suppose some object further that the scriptures never directly specify that children should be baptized. In that case, we should note that the scriptures do not specify that women should participate in Holy Communion. But obviously, Christian women should commune, as has been the church's practice from day one. Peter noted that the promise was to adults and their children (Acts 2:39). Hence, baptisms in the ancient church included entire households. Once the head of the family sought baptism, the entire household, including the spouse, children, servants, and the servants' children, were baptized (Acts 16:15). Jesus makes it clear that children can and do believe (Matt 18:6). And, if children could become members of the old covenant through circumcision, it makes no sense that the new covenant would be less generous. Given our culture's tendency to focus on autonomy, we have a hard time acknowledging along with Jesus how God works in the life of a child. Though written decades ago, the thoughts of Royal F. Peterson are still pertinent:

> The soul of a child does not exercise an active response in the manner of an adult. The soul of a child is passive and receptive. It knows nothing of the doubts and struggles of a later age. It offers no resistance to the work of the Spirit of God. The heart of a child is a fertile field in which the Holy Spirit can sow the seed of faith freely. It becomes quite clear, therefore, why Jesus could speak of "these little ones who believe in me" (Matt. 18:6). The presence of the Holy Spirit makes the passive heart of a child a yielded heart.[1]

Infant baptism is a perfect acknowledgment that the whole person of believers is upheld in God's hands. More than anything, infant baptism shows us that we

---

[1] Royal F. Peterson, *Baptized into Christ* (Rock Island, Illinois: Augustana Press, 1959), 30.

are most assured of our salvation when our faith is directed not to our cognitive faculties, emotional inner compass, or sincere acts of piety but instead to God's merciful and gracious favor granted to us in baptism, a mercy beyond our abilities to fathom.

Conclusion

How can I know if I'm saved? Should I look for new affections as an indicator? Should I look to new behaviors? Should I look to a decision for Christ that I've made? No. It's Jesus' decision that counts: "You did not choose me, but I chose you and appointed you that you should go and bear fruit . . . " (John 15:16). When Christ comes into our lives, we should expect new motives, new desires, and a new will to appear. Christ acquits us of our sin and renews us, making us new creatures. He gives us a new birth. He does so through each day, drowning the old being and, by means of the Word, the life-evoking promise given in our baptisms, calling new men and women to come forth. That said, the foundation of our salvation is not to be found in this newness, no matter how exciting it might be. After all, we continue to wrestle with the old Adam or Eve. There will always be an element of ambiguity in the Christian life until the old being is completely dead and we are welcomed into heaven.

Faith can live with that tension. You should never beat yourself up for your imperfections or whether or not your repentance is sincere or thorough enough. God is not finished with you yet. But can you be sure you are saved? Absolutely! Christ has given you a right to heaven. It is yours to claim. It's given as a gift. You haven't earned it or deserved it. But in faith, you are cemented to Christ. You can be sure if you've gotten the Word of the One whose promises are sure. His reliability is our only real assurance. His destiny, heaven, is yours as well.

Acknowledgments

I'm very grateful to the following who generously gave of their time and skill to comment on and suggest improvements for this booklet: Ken Sundet Jones, Jarle Blindheim, Bob Kolb, John Pless, Jarrod Thomas, Brent Kuhlman, Jamie Strickler, Russ and Abby Lackey, Dennis Nelson, Jack Kilcrease, and Rick Ritchie.

More Best Sellers from

Find these titles
and more at 1517.org/**shop**

Never Go Another Day Without Hearing the Gospel of Jesus.

Visit **www.1517.org**
for free Gospel resources.